ABOUT] MOUNTAIN MEADOWS FAMILY MASSACRE

ENDORSEMENTS

Family traditions and stories are sometimes lost or forgotten with the passing of years when they are not written for future generations. *Murder in the Mountains: The Justus and Meadows Family Massacre* is the true story of a family tragedy that will never be forgotten. The heartbreak caused by this awful deed is now documented for family, friends, and neighbors as well as for those who have heard the story at some time in their life. In addition, Georgia Charles lays the groundwork for her book by familiarizing her readers with the way of life in the mountains. While progress has made its way to this remote area, it has not spoiled the simple heart-felt love of family and friends. While tragedy breaks the hearts of those left behind, it also draws them closer, knitting their souls with a bond that lasts forever. Hospitality and friendliness still reign, for when people share a common bond—when they've gone through tough times together—they are stronger and more compassionate.

—Joyce Ann Rose, Author of *The Potter's House*

I was deeply moved by the author's drive and devotion to finally let her family and friends see, through her thoughts and grief, the sadness of what happened to their family by documenting the blood bath of her precious ancestors. *Murder in the Mountains: The Justus and Meadows Family Massacre* tells the story of a family torn apart because of one man's greed! A must read!

—Gilda Rose, Author of *Playmates from Heaven*

MURDER

IN THE MOUNTAINS

MURDER
IN THE MOUNTAINS

The Justus and Meadows Family Massacre

GEORGIA CHARLES

YorkshirePublishing
www.yorkshirepublishing.com
Write Now.

ISBN: 978-1-947825-61-1

Murder in the Mountains

Copyright © 2013 by Georgia Charles

Yorkshire Publishing
3207 South Norwood Avenue
Tulsa, Oklahoma 74135
www.YorkshirePublishing.com
918.394.2665

ACKNOWLEDGMENTS

I have spent the last few years searching for information about the murders of my ancestors and talked to many relatives who have shared with me their stories and recollections from their immediate descendants. Others have provided assistance, guidance, and resources that have been invaluable to me in completing this book. I would like to acknowledge and give thanks to everyone who gave of their time and memories to help me with this project. I especially want to say thanks to Roseann (Charles) Matney for graciously allowing me to spend time with her and listen to her stories. Thanks also to Susan Slone Sturgill, one of my Charles cousins, who helped tremendously by giving me access to her years of genealogy research. I would also like to thank Georgia (Blankenship) Robair-West for many delightful evenings in her home sharing her family history with me, through which I found another family connection to Grandma Elizabeth. A special thank you to Lisa Jetts with the Washington County Virginia Public Library for her guidance toward various sources to search for information as well as graciously and patiently answering so many questions. To Gilda Rose, author of *Playmates from Heaven* and Joyce Ann Rose, author of *The Potters House:* thanks to each of you for your expert insight and guidance into the world of book publishing. I couldn't have done it without you.

Paul, an apostle, (not of men, neither by man, but by Jesus Christ, and God the Father, who raised him from the dead;) And all the brethren which are with me, unto the churches of Galatia, Grace be to you and peace from God the Father, and from our Lord Jesus Christ, Who gave himself for our sins, that he might deliver us from this present evil world, according to the will of God and our Father: To whom be glory for ever and ever. Amen.

Galatians 1:1-5 KJV

INTRODUCTION

This story has been with me since I was a young girl growing up in Hurley, Virginia. I have never been able to get the story out of my mind for long. I have always felt the story of these tragedies needed to be told; and, as a direct descendant, that a family member could give more insight into how it affected the family. My dream has always been to share this story, but to be truthful, I never knew how this would happen. I never considered myself a writer, but always felt that the history of what happened to these wonderful people should be documented and never forgotten, especially by the family and the generations that followed. This has been a book in progress for many years. I did not want to start upon this journey until I felt I had accumulated as much documentation as possible to tell the story of what happened accurately and to the best of my ability.

My goal was to gather information from documented sources, to be as factually correct as possible, and to accurately convey the story as it happened. With the tremendous help of the Internet, social media and electronic information sharing, it is so much easier to gather information today than it was years ago. There was a book written approximately thirty years ago by George W. Stacy titled *The Man from Knox Creek*, which told the story of the murders. I read the book many years ago. The story tells some of what happened, and some things I remember being told to me as a child, yet I have attempted to compile more factual documentation in order to present a clearer picture of how and why (as much as possible) this crime occurred.

THE HURLEY COMMUNITY

The community of Hurley is located in the Knox Creek section of Buchanan County, Virginia, in the far southwest corner of the Commonwealth of Virginia. Hurley is bordered by Kentucky and West Virginia. The terrain of the area is mountainous and remote. In this part of Buchanan County, there are sheer cliffs and towering ridges that frame an immense sky. The community has an IGA Grocery Store, a pharmacy, a medical clinic, a Dollar General Store, post office, bank, and a great family restaurant. The town seat of Buchanan County is located in Grundy, about a forty-five-minute drive from Hurley. In the far corners of Hurley (near the Kentucky or West Virginia line), it can be as much as a one- and one-half-hour drive to Grundy. From any direction, residents must drive over mountains to get to town. It is a way of life, and the people in Hurley will tell you they would not have it any other way. For the majority of their needs, residents go to Grundy for grocery shopping, hospital, doctor visits, pharmacies, funeral homes, restaurants, movies, and other social outings.

Walmart opened in Grundy in August 2011. Before the Walmart opened, Buchanan County residents drove to the nearest Walmart in Pikeville, Kentucky, or Claypool Hill, Virginia. For larger shopping excursions, residents travel to Bristol, Virginia; Johnson City, Tennessee; Roanoke, Virginia; and Lexington, Kentucky.

The opening of Walmart had long been anticipated, as the town of Grundy was demolished about 2002 due to the flooding of the Levisa River and had been in the reconstruction phase since. The town was taken down and rebuilt on the other side of the Levisa River as a means of avoiding damages to businesses when the Levisa overflows. It will be a beautiful town and place to live once the construction is completed and other businesses come to the area. Grundy has the Appalachian School of Law and Appalachian College of Pharmacy. Also expected to open in the fall of 2014 is the Appalachian College of Optometry These colleges have been a boon to the town and bring students from across Virginia and other states to complete a higher education. Students enjoy lower tuition and housing rates and a small-town-community way of life while getting a quality education.

This is the true story about the murders of my great-grandmother Elizabeth (Baker) Justus; her youngest daughter, Lydia (Justus) Meadows; son-in-law George Meadows; and three small sons of George and Lydia, Noah, Lafayette, and Will Meadows (in birth order). The murders occurred one fall evening, it has been said, between 9:00 and 10:00 p.m. on September 21, 1909. Elizabeth was known as Aunt Betty in the Hurley community. I will hereafter refer to her by that title. As a side note, the surname Justus has been spelled differently in various documents. I have seen it spelled Justice and Justis. Our ancestors spelled the last name Justus. Aunt Betty and most of her children lived in the Laurel Creek section of Hurley. Off the main road going into the town of Hurley, you follow a curvy road back into Laurel Creek for about one or two miles to Aunt Betty's home place.

After the death of her husband, Hiram Wylie Justus, Aunt Betty's youngest daughter, Lydia, her husband George, and the three young boys lived in the home with her. It was a peaceful, quiet, and simple life. A lot of the history has been handed down from older family members through the generations as well as historical data, documented information from various sources, documents, and Internet sites. Mary Polly (Justus) Charles was Aunt Betty's daughter and my paternal grandmother. Polly's son, Daniel, was my father. Over the years, there have been several articles written about the murders by various authors. I have always felt it was important for a direct descendant to share our side of the story, to give the family's perspective and tell the stories that were handed down through the generations.

Aunt Betty was born in Pike County, Kentucky, in April 1843. She married Hiram Wylie Justus on March 8, 1860.

Hiram was born in Tazewell County, Virginia, on October 15, 1837. He was a private in the Confederate States Army, Wells Co Smiths BN VA CAV. Hiram was a farmer when he was not off with the army. To them were born twelve children: Matilda, who died in infancy; MacDaniel (called Daniel); Amy Caroline (Justus) Blankenship; Mary Polly (Justus) Charles; Morgan; Samuel Senna; Alfred; James; Lafayette; Pricy Jane (Justus) Baker; Lewis Wayne; Andrew; and Lydia (Justus) Meadows. Hiram and Aunt Betty eventually settled in Buchanan County, Virginia, in the Knox Creek area and lived on Laurel Fork of Knox Creek and raised their family in this community.

I have been told that Aunt Betty loved to work in her garden and that she loved her flowers. She had beautiful flowers of all kinds planted around her home—rose bushes, marigolds, daffodils, tulips, and all kinds of flowering bushes. She also had an orchard with lots of fruit trees. In my mind's eye, I can picture the cabin surrounded by ancient oaks, poplars, maple, and probably paw paw trees, as well as beautiful flowers everywhere. During my mother's, Rosie Stacy Charles, lifetime, especially when she was younger, she was very knowledgeable about mountain medicine, gathering roots and herbs to use for medicinal purposes. I am sure the same would be true for Aunt Betty and her daughters as well. My mother would tell me how herbs and plants were used for medicinal concoctions. She would say they were provided to us by God for our use in healing. Nightshade plants, when powdered and combined with creams to make a liniment, were good for poison ivy. Another remedy would be to use nightshade and yellow dock plants to make a liniment for snakebite! To the old timers, every plant was used to cure most any ailment. The use of feverweed mixed with gin was used to break a fever; hive weed was used, of course, to cure hives! Powdered alum mixed with yellow root would cure thrash or "white tongue." Nettle root was used to ease the pain of measles; salve made from ginseng was used for age spots; sweet fennel was used to make the house smell good, and fennel will also get rid of fleas! Of course, you have to know how to mix the concoctions and have the correct amounts to mix together, and any other extra ingredient that need to go into the medicine. My mom also liked to use sassafras tea for colds and flu. A side benefit is the wonderful aroma, and it makes the house smell great. Mom always said herbs and roots had a lot of healing powers. Mom also learned from Grandma Polly to make a tea for babies to cure colds and flu. It was made from the catnip plant, boiled down and sweetened. Both Mom and Grandma Polly also like to use marigolds to make salve.

Hiram Wylie Justus died February 21, 1903. Both he and Aunt Betty are buried on Laurel Creek in the Justus Family Cemetery. The cemetery is about three hundred yards from the site of the home place, a log cabin. Nine of their children are also buried on Laurel Creek. The other children are buried in the Hurley area. Grandma Polly is buried in the

Charles Family Cemetery on Straight Fork of the Blackey area of Hurley, just a few miles from Laurel Creek.

In the early 1900s, the citizens of the Hurley community were close-knit families, relatives, and neighbors. It was the kind of community (and still is to this day) where your neighbors were like family. For the most part, everyone knew everyone else in the community, and there really were not a lot of strangers unknown to the people of the area. It was a great place to live. People raised their families mainly by farming and raising animals. Their livelihood also included game hunting, fishing, gathering fruits and nuts, and preserving foods grown from the farms for the winter. Families always put up canned peaches, apples, pears, and other delicious fruits. These were also dried as a method of preservation.

I remember as a child in the summer some of our chores were to go to the fields and pick strawberries, blackberries, and blueberries. Of course, I ate about as many as I picked because they were delicious! My mother always made jams, jellies, and preserves from them. They were sure appreciated on cold winter mornings when Mom made fresh-baked biscuits. There was nothing better than putting homemade cow's butter on the biscuit and slathering it with the homemade preserves.

It was common during this era for people to have large families. I am sure it helped to have a lot of children who would grow up and help keep the farms going. It also meant there was a lot of family in your life, from children to grandchildren, aunts, uncles, and cousins. There was always some family member close by, and you had the pleasure of knowing that you had a lot of places to visit because family was always near. The way we grew up, there was no fear of violence or a child being stolen or molested. Our parents did not have to worry about a child being out of their sight for a couple hours. They knew other family members were always around and would look after the children.

Aunt Betty was a midwife, and many family members have said that she delivered a lot of babies in the Hurley community during her lifetime. She also taught her daughter, Grandma Polly, to be a midwife. Polly got her certification and basically took over from Aunt Betty and, in her lifetime, delivered a lot of babies in Hurley. Grandma Polly also delivered most of her own grandchildren. When I was a little girl, I remember my Dad telling me that Grandma Polly would get on her horse any time of the day or night and go where she was needed to deliver a baby. He also told me that Grandma Polly said there were times during winter when she would ride her horse to deliver a baby, and it would be so cold, her boots would freeze to the stirrups! My parents had eleven children, and Grandma Polly delivered eight of them. She passed away before the last three children were born. Mom's last three children— my sister Texie, brother Oliver, and myself—were delivered at home by Doc Richardson.

Hear me when I call, O God of my righteousness:
thou hast enlarged me when I was in distress; have
mercy upon me, and hear my prayer.

Psalms 4:1 KJV

AUNT BETTY'S ADVENTURES
AND OTHER STORIES

During the early 1900s, Hurley was a thriving community and at that time was intended to be the county seat. There was Hurley Hospital (also referred to as the Knox Creek Hospital) with at least one doctor and several nurses for the hospital. However, because of the remoteness of the area, the county seat was moved to Grundy. During this time, W. M. Ritter Lumber Company was a thriving business in Hurley. Ritter Lumber was a timber and logging company and made Hurley the center of operations, with four divisions throughout the Hurley area. Once the timber was cut and processed, it was sent by the Big Sandy and Cumberland Railroad that met up with the Norfolk and Western Pocahontas line at Devon, West Virginia. In addition to farming, most of the men in the community worked for the W. M. Ritter Lumber Company at one time or another.

Some family history was shared with me by one of my cousins, Roseann Charles Matney. Roseann is the daughter of McClellan "Clell" and Pricey Charles. Clell was my uncle, a son of Adam and Polly Charles. Roseann tells the story of a time when Hiram was off with the army, and Aunt Betty decided she wanted to go visit her family either in Kentucky or near the Ohio River. She loaded up two horses and a cow. One of the horses was used to carry their belongings and the other used for Aunt Betty and some of the children to ride. The cow was brought for milk for them and also for one of her little children. Her oldest son, Daniel, went with her. It took a long time to get to the Ohio River. The story is told that she killed a large black bear on her way to Ohio. Other family members say that an infant child died along the way. However, I am not sure how accurate this information is when looking at the dates of birth and death of her children. Her first child, Matilda, died as an infant. Aunt Betty and her children eventually made it to her family and spent a good deal of time visiting with them. She then journeyed back to her home in Hurley. Some older ancestors have recollected that Aunt Betty was a small, petite woman but that she was tough and independent-minded and could well take care of herself. The elder family members (long gone now) who remembered her spoke fondly of Aunt Betty as being a wonderful lady, very warmhearted and a wonderful mother and grandmother. She was the type of person who never met a stranger, and anyone who came to her home was treated like family. Unfortunately, there are no pictures of her that I have been able to locate. There is a sketch made that supposedly was of her likeness (my best educated guess is that the sketch was made by an artist for the *Master Detective* article). I am not sure how accurate the sketch really is. I remember my Aunt Caroline telling me that her mother, Polly (my grandmother), looked a lot like Aunt Betty. I have included a picture of Grandma Polly to show how Aunt Betty possibly looked. Grandma was also a petite and feisty lady!

Roseann tells the story that was passed on to her by her parents, Clell and Pricey Charles. One time Aunt Betty came to visit at Clell and Pricey's homeplace up on Straight Fork. My grandparents Adam and Mary Polly (Justus) Charles also came along on the visit to spend a few days as well. She said that when everyone had gone to bed one night, there was the sound of a large bird screeching in the house. The family said there was no way a bird could have gotten into the house because the doors and windows were closed. After searching the house, they did not see nor could they find the bird. They only heard the loud screeching sound that went on for a long time.

Another story goes that Aunt Betty was spending time at my grandparents' house, Adam and Polly. In the tradition of large families, at the end of the evening after all the chores were done and supper was finished, all the family gathered on the large front porch to talk about their day and their lives in general. Well, this particular evening when all the family was gathered together, there came the sound of horses and people going down the road. The horses were running at full speed, and the people were shouting. The family became frightened because, even though they could hear the horses' hooves pounding the dirt road and people shouting, there was no one there. They could not see anyone! After the heinous murders, the family felt this was certainly a premonition of things to come.

The home of my grandparents eventually became the home of my parents, Daniel and Rosie Charles. I was born in this home, and it is still the only place I call home today. The home is over one hundred years old.

Another story goes that during this same time when Aunt Betty was staying with Grandma Polly, they went for a walk one night before bedtime. They were walking along a path, and Aunt Betty was telling Grandma Polly that she had enough money to take care of her for a long time, and none of the children would have to be burdened about taking care of her. Grandma Polly supposedly kept shushing Aunt Betty, telling her to be quiet and to not talk about that, because someone might hear her.

Aunt Betty and Hiram Wylie had about 150 acres of mountain land on Laurel Creek, and there was a large amount of timber on her property. After Hiram died, Aunt Betty decided to sell some of the timber. In July 1909, she sold a large tract of the timberland to the W. M. Ritter Lumber Company. I suppose she either walked or rode her horse to the offices of the Ritter Lumber Company to make the transaction. According to the story in the July 1935 edition of *Master Detective*, "Capturing the Killer of the Cumberlands," Aunt Betty walked into the Ritter offices, and the tall man standing over a high desk counted out the crisp bills to her, a total of $1,300.00. The man was Howard Little, purchasing agent for the W. M. Ritter Lumber Company.

Mr. Little remarked to Aunt Betty, "Plenty hot out for anyone like you to be traveling."

Aunt Betty retorted, "Ain't nothin' at all for me. I'm as hard as nails."

Mr. Little then told Aunt Betty to be careful with all that money. "That's a fortune around these parts."

Aunt Betty replied, "Don't you worry none about me. I can take care of myself."

On her way back to her home, because it was so hot, she stopped along the way at several neighbors' farms to rest a spell and get a drink of water. Neighbors asked, "What are you doing out on the road in the middle of the day in this heat?"

Aunt Betty told them about the sale of her timber and that she was on the way home with her money. "I'm going to put it in a safe place where no one can get at it," she said in between taking puffs from her pipe. "I know how to take care of things."

The family history goes that she added the money from the sale of the timber with other money that she had saved. Some said she carried some of the money on her person, in a money belt. Family lore also says she supposedly buried some of the money in the backyard. Still others say some of the cash was placed in a metal milk pail and buried in a dug-out place made under the grate, which was used for making fires and for warmth during winter months. This dug out was made especially to bury or hide things to keep them safe and so no one would find what you wanted to keep hidden.

Aunt Betty lived on Laurel Creek, and several of her grown children and their families lived nearby. They were a very close-knit family, and they looked out for each other. I remember my dad telling me as a young girl that one of her older sons was away from home on a trip for a few days and that the murders happened while he was away. (Some believe her oldest son, Daniel, was considered more of the protector of the family, and he was away. After reading the *Master Detective* article, my thoughts were that it might have been her son, Senna or Sennitt, who was away from home. He was married to Lilabelle Justus, and she appears to be the first to know what happened; however, Senna is not mentioned.) The family believed that the man who committed the murders knew the older son was away and felt this was the time to do what he intended to do and that he would have a better opportunity to commit the crime and get away with it. The family also believed it was possible that the intent was to rob Aunt Betty of her money and not necessarily to murder anyone. My dad told me that most of his family, Grandma Polly and Grandpa Adam, and his other brothers and sisters believed it was a robbery gone wrong. However, this person probably did not anticipate the difficulty he would have in trying to steal money from someone and get away with it. Something went terribly wrong on Laurel Creek on that fall night in 1909.

For, behold, the Lord cometh forth out of his place,
and will come down, and tread upon the high places
of the earth.

Micah 1:3, KJV

A SCENE OF HORROR

September 21, 1909, was a cool fall evening and, I imagine, the family of Aunt Betty, her daughter Lydia, son-in-law George Meadows, and their three small sons, Noah, Will, and Lafayette, spent a normal evening together. The family history says that the person who murdered them was known to them, most likely as a friend, as well as a member of the community. My dad, aunts, and uncles believed he came to their home and asked to spend the night. This was not uncommon during this time for someone to spend the night at another person's home, especially if they were a distance from their own dwelling. A family would think nothing of offering that person the hospitality of their home, a meal, and a bed for the night, and they would be on their way the next day.

The family legend says that after everyone was in bed that night, this person attempted to find the money Aunt Betty had, and he intended to steal the money and be on his way. We will never know exactly what transpired inside the home that night. If the intent was to only steal the money, something went horribly wrong, and the theft was fouled. It would appear that the family, maybe Aunt Betty herself, was not asleep and became aware of what their lodger intended. The family interrupted the thief in his attempt to find the money. Most likely, the son-in-law, George Meadows, and probably the adult women attempted to fight off the lodger and get him out of the house. In the *Master Detective* article, dated July 1935, A. C. Hufford, the detective who investigated the murder, told the story to John E. Bailey, the author of the article. The article is titled "Capturing the Killer of the Cumberlands." Detective Hufford's theory was that everyone had gone to bed that night, and the murderer came knocking at the door. This theory is based on the fact that when George Meadows was found, he was dressed in his nightshirt. Detective Hufford theorized that George Meadows went to answer the door and was shot by the murderer. We may never know exactly how it happened, but it seems that with this theory, the time line is off. If the murderer came to the door and George Meadows answered the door, and the killer shot George Meadows twice, he would not have had time to kill the other family members, burn down the house, and escape before Aunt Betty's other children and/or neighbors who lived nearby heard the shots and came to check on the family. It seems more likely that the murderer was a guest with the family for the night, as told in family lore through the generations. The family members most likely fought with the murderer. He killed everyone inside the house except for George Meadows, who attempted to get out of the house, possibly with one of the children, and was shot and killed outside the house. The murderer then most likely set the house on fire, thinking all evidence would be erased if everyone was burned up, and then escaped before family members could get to the home.

What we know is that everyone was brutally murdered and the house was then set on fire. In the early morning hours, other family members who lived close by heard two shots ring out and went to investigate. They became aware that Aunt Betty's house was burning. When they got to the home, to their horror, they discovered that all family members were dead. The home was in ashes, and Aunt Betty's family (sons, daughters, sons-in-law, daughters-in-law, and grandchildren) discovered the bodies of Aunt Betty, Lydia, and the three children. They had been the victims of a gruesome and brutal murder. The family wondered where George Meadows was. Had he gone mad and murdered everyone and set the house on fire? George Meadows's body, however, was soon discovered outside the home, with two bullet wounds to the body and three gaping cuts in the head and neck. The charred remains of his youngest son, Lafayette, were found under what was left of the front steps.

Family history believes George Meadows attempted to get out of the house and grabbed the child nearest him. In going out of the house, he was fatally attacked with some weapon. Maybe he was still alive, and the only other option for the murderer was to shoot to kill George. Detective Hufford states that all family members had been decapitated. Roseann Charles Matney stated that, according to the family history told to her by her mother, George Meadows's body was found outside. His head, supposedly, rolled down the yard into the garden. She stated that the home was situated on a hill, and the yard was sloping down toward the garden. When the bodies of the other family members were discovered, their skulls were found away from the rest of their charred bodies in the smoldering ashes of the home.

The following information is from the July, 1935 *Master Detective* article, "Capturing the Killer of the Cumberlands."

> Lilabelle Justus, or "Lillie," was a daughter-in-law, married to Sennitt or "Senna" Justus, one of Aunt Betty's sons. She states in the article that she stirred restlessly in her sleep as she lay in bed in her frame house three hundred yards down the valley from where Aunt Betty lived. Suddenly two shots shattered the midnight stillness. A woman's scream split the air. Her heart pounding wildly, Lillie Justus sat up in bed and listened. An orange glow was reflected in the bedroom. Lillie pulled a coat over her nightdress and ran out of the house. Angry tongues of flame were licking at the air from the roof of Aunt Betty's house, and a whirling mass of cinders shot skyward amid a puff of black smoke. Up the rocky creek bed Lillie stumbled, heedless

of the jagged stones that cut her bare feet. The front door of Aunt Betty's house was swung open, revealing a roaring hell inside. Lillie shielded her face and struggled to approach. There, in the swirl of flames, she saw the burning body of Aunt Betty lying on the floor. A few feet away lay the body of Lydia, and, close to her as if seeking protection, were two of Lydia's small boys. Lillie Justus turned away, sickened at the sight. Soon other family members and neighbors were tumbling out of bed, attracted by the roaring, crackling flames, and soon the little yard in front of the house was filled with trampling feet. The rugged faces of the hill people were grave as they gazed upon the scene of horror. Before long they found the body of George Meadows lying against the yard palings. Squire P. L. Johnson, a sheriff's deputy in the Hurley area, was notified and arrived at the scene of the crime as soon as possible.

The next day, September 22, Detective A. C. Hufford from Bluefield, West Virginia, was contacted by Chief Robert Thornton.[1] Chief Thornton stated to Detective Hufford that there had been a terrible crime committed in Hurley, over in Buchanan County, Virginia, and that they didn't have a lot of details yet but asked Detective Hufford to go at once and make a thorough investigation. The detective made the next train over the Norfolk

---

[1] Some have indicated that he was with The Pinkerton Agency but I have not been able to verify the information.

and Western to Devon, West Virginia, and from there rode the Big Sandy & Cumberland Railroad, on a rattling, narrow-gauge lumber road into Grundy, Virginia. Detective Hufford first examined the body of George Meadows. There were two bullet wounds in the body and three gaping cuts in the head and neck. It appeared the latter had been inflicted with a sharp instrument, such as a hatchet. The yard surrounding the charred home was trampled, and anything that might have given a lead was obliterated. The detective ordered that the bodies of the victims be removed from the smoking ruins. Then another horrible discovery was made. Under what was left of the front steps, the body of little Lafayette, the youngest member of the family, was found. His puny body was burned almost beyond recognition, the sixth victim of the ruthless killer. The skulls of some of the bodies found in the ruins had been split by a sharp instrument, and the head of each had been completely severed.

On every side, murder was evident, and neighbors eagerly relayed to Detective Hufford about the money (stated as $1,300.00) Aunt Betty was reputed to have hidden in the house. The motive appeared clear. Now the question was, who was the killer? The meager evidence at hand indicated that someone well acquainted with the family might have committed the crime, but so well had the killer covered his tracks with fire that no clue was left. Detective Hufford states that he went into the blackened building and poked among the debris. After a careful search, he was rewarded by finding a hatchet, and he believed that to be the murder weapon. Going over the place inch by inch, he tried to picture the circumstances surrounding the crime. He had the bullets removed from George Meadows's body and found that they had been fired from a .32-20 caliber gun. They were lead slugs and, although fired at close range, had failed to go through the body. A systematic check was made of all firearms in the community to determine, if possible, who owned a gun of that caliber. After searching the homes of many of the hill farmers, a man named McClanahan was located who owned a .32-20 Winchester Special revolver. McClanahan said determinedly, while whittling on a stick, that he lost that confounded gun about two months before while he was down in West Virginia. Taken before Squire P. L. Johnson, he repeated his story. The sole promising clue led to disappointment. Suggestions from all quarters were given careful consideration, but to no avail. Finally, as a last resort, they decided to use bloodhounds. A special train was put into service on the B. S. & C. Railroad and was soon worming its way down the narrow valley of Knox Creek to Devon, West Virginia. Communication facilities were not very advanced in this section at that time, and that was the best that could be done.

From Devon, a telephone message was sent to Mr. David Wolford in Kentucky who owned a pack of hounds. But by the time he could make his way over the rough mountain roads to the train and complete the journey to Hurley, more than thirty-six hours had elapsed, and the trails had grown cold. However, a half-dozen dogs were soon sniffing eagerly about the yard surrounding the burned dwelling. Back and forth they dashed and for a time seemed bewildered. At last one of the animals gave an excited bark and started the rest on a trail up the mountainside, through a clearing, and then into a dense, tangled forest. Onward they went, yelping madly and dragging their master and the rest of the search party through a dark ravine. Up they climbed to the top of a hogback ridge, and after following along this for a short distance, they turned down the rough, steep mountain toward the smoke-filled valley below. The search party eagerly followed, hoping that at the end of the rough trail lay the solution to the murder mystery. Straight ahead they were led to a cabin, the home of Lewis Justus, a mountaineer.[2] All the men had guns drawn, and their faces were grim as they faced the door. The door opened slowly, and a gaunt, tanned face with a stubble of beard looked out. It was Lewis himself.

"What's wrong, boys?" he inquired, his eyes shifting from the dogs to the men with guns. "Are you looking for somebody?"

---

[2] A different Lewis Justus, not Aunt Betty's son.

"We're looking for you," Detective Hufford stated. "What do you know about the killings down in Laurel Creek?"

Lewis shook his head from side to side. "Boys," he said solemnly, "I guess I've been pretty tough playing cards, drinking and all, but upon my honor, I hain't never killed no widder like Aunt Betty."

Lewis ambled out from the shelter of the door, the hounds sniffing eagerly at his heels. Following him came his equally gaunt and angular son, Ephraim. Both men were placed under arrest and taken down to Squire Johnson.

Lewis maintained, "I wasn't nigh Aunt Betty's around the time of the fire. I was playing a game of stud poker on the night of the twenty-first."

Ephraim said the same thing. To sustain their story, they produced witnesses, the men with whom they had played cards on the night in question, and their alibi was ironclad. It was proven that they had no connection with the crime, and they were subsequently released.

Mr. Wolford was paid for the service of the dogs and returned to Kentucky. Every clue had been exhausted and no nearer the solution of the mystery than when first started. Detective Hufford decided to make an attempt to identify the money that Aunt Betty had been paid for her timber. Perhaps the Ritter Lumber Company had recorded the serial numbers of the bills. It was a long chance but worth taking.

The detective made his way over the rough trails to the logging camps of the Ritter Lumber Company, far up in the hills. He knew the purchasing agent, Howard Little, stayed there the greater part of the time and wanted to talk to him about the money. But when he arrived, to his disappointment, he learned from the loggers that Little had resigned and had left two weeks before. One of the lumberjacks volunteered that Little said he was going west as soon as he could get things straightened out. Detective Hufford asked the men where Little could be located now. The lumberjacks looked at each other, grinning slyly.

One of the younger men chuckled. "I guess Mary Stacy over to Green Collins's place knows enough about him," he said, with amused glances at his companions.

Collins was a farmer living a short distance out of Hurley. The detective decided to go there to find out where to get in touch with Little, hoping that he would be able to throw some light on the case. He found the unpainted rambling structure that housed the Collins family. Collins himself was seated on the porch, puffing away on a corncob pipe. He said nothing, his teeth clamped firmly on the stem of his pipe.

Detective Hufford asked Collins, "Do you know Howard Little, the purchasing agent up at the Ritter mill?"

"Maybe," Collins replied.

"Do you know where he is now?" Hufford asked.

"No, I don't," he replied.

The detective noticed that the man was unusually quiet. He went into the house and found Mrs. Collins and Mary Stacy busy with the washing. They, too, were reluctant to talk about Mr. Little, the Stacy girl coloring crimson at the mention of his name. The detective decided to take them before Squire Johnson for questioning, and after much persuasion, they agreed to go. Mary Stacy was the first to be put on the stand. A lithe-limbed mountain creature, she was in the full bloom of youth. After stating that she knew nothing about Howard Little's affairs, she finally admitted that they were lovers.

"He used to come down to see me a few times a week," she said, "but lately I have missed him."

While she was testifying, Mrs. Collins, a thin, worn woman, sat constantly smoothing out her faded gingham dress. When it came her turn to take the stand, her lips twitched nervously. Squire Johnson began to question her in a stern voice, and her apprehension increased. She darted quick glances at her husband, who sat staring at her.

"When was the last time you saw Howard Little?" thundered Johnson.

Mrs. Collins trembled and gripped the arms of the witness chair. "I can't keep this up," she said, her voice shaking. "I saw him about the seventh of September. He gave Mary Stacy fifteen dollars and told her to get some clothes. They were going on a long trip, he said."

"Did he say where they were going?"

Nervously fingering her dress and avoiding the blazing glances of Mary Stacy, she continued, "Yes. He said he had some money in a bank at Bluefield, and as soon as he could get it, they would go out West."

"How much money?" asked Squire Johnson.

"Thirteen hundred dollars," replied Mrs. Collins.

Was it possible that Little, the trusted mill agent, was involved? Detective Hufford arranged for a man from his Bluefield office to investigate Little's bank account. Word came back that he had no account. What was his motive then in lying to Mary Stacy? Why had he hit upon the damning sum of $1,300.00? The detective determined at any cost to question Little himself and sent a man to inquire of the merchants in Bluefield as to his whereabouts. In a short while, he reported that Little had gone back to his farm at Alnwick, West Virginia.[3]

Robert Bailey, a farmer who often did confidential work for Detective Hufford's agency, went to the Little home in the guise of a sheep buyer. He found the tall, thin Howard Little lying disconsolately on a cot, his trousers rolled up, revealing one of his legs wrapped in dirty bandages.

---

[3] This area is believed to be bordered on the Virginia and West Virginia line.

"I'm aiming to buy some of your sheep," said Bailey after he introduced himself.

Little raised himself up on his elbow and then sank back with a groan. "I can't do a thing while I've got this blasted leg," he said, gritting his teeth. "You'll have to wait until I get better before I can do any business with you."

"That's too bad about your leg," sympathized Bailey. "How did it happen?"

"I tried to cut a tree that had come down in the road," Little replied, turning his face toward the wall.

Bailey pressed the subject no further, but when he took his leave, he decided to see the tree in question. As his horse picked it way over the stony, creek-bed road, Bailey wondered whether the cut on Little's leg bore any relation to the severed heads of the murder victims back in Hurley. Finally he reached the spot where the tree was supposed to have fallen. It was dried and weather-beaten and had been down at least two years. No axe marks were on it.

Bailey made his report to Detective Hufford, who began to sum things up. The lie about the bank account, the lie about the cut leg, the hatchet wounds on the victims, and the hatchet found in the ruins all served to strengthen the growing suspicions about Howard Little. Hufford immediately communicated with the West Virginia authorities and asked them to arrest and hold Little in connection with the killings in Hurley. Meanwhile, information came that showed that Little had a .32-20 caliber revolver in his possession at the time of the murders. It had been loaned to him by Noah Stacy, a bartender in an Alnwick saloon. Stacy relayed that the gun had been found by his younger brother some time before, but as his father objected to the youth keeping it, Stacy had held it at the saloon. About a week before the murders, he had loaned the gun to Little, who claimed that he wanted to kill a dog that had been harassing his sheep.

When Little was taken into custody, he was questioned on that point but denied having touched a gun for the past three years. Detective Hufford continued the investigation and found that the gun had been returned to Stacy's father on the Sunday following the killings. Two empty shells were in the chamber. George Meadows had been shot twice. Little was taken to Bluefield, West Virginia, and placed in jail. His demeanor was cool, and he confidently waived extradition proceedings. Taken back to Virginia, he was placed in the Russell County Jail at Lebanon.

Back in Hurley, the hill folk were excitedly discussing the capture. A crowd was gathered about the post office when the news came in. "He ought to be lynched," said one of the older men as he waved a newspaper in the air. The crowd echoed the same thoughts. With memories of the brutal slaughter of six innocent persons still fresh in their minds, an embittered band of mountaineers left Hurley one starlit night in October. Swiftly they rode down upon the seat of justice in Russell County. Wires were cut along the route in order that no message of warning might precede them and frustrate their plans.

There was a sharp clatter of horses' hooves down the street in Lebanon, and the jailer peered from a window in the stone building. His face blanched when he saw gun muzzles pointed toward him.

"Don't shoot!" he screamed as he hurried to open the door. In a few minutes, he was stripped of his keys by the determined raiders, and they hurriedly swung back the massive iron doors of the prison proper. On they went through the dimly lit hall, their heavy boots pounding like the hooves of a herd of wild horses. Stopping in front of the solid steel door that barred Little's cell, they inserted the key and threw open the door with a clang. Like a pack of hungry wolves eager to be at their prey, they pushed into the cell. It was empty. Little was gone! Years later, the raiders learned that in their haste they had forgotten about the branch telephone line, which made a circuitous route into the county seat. It was over this line that the authorities in Lebanon had been notified of their coming and, thus forewarned, had removed Little to a place of safety.

Detective Hufford questioned Mrs. Little, who was not at home at the time of the arrest. She was a small, thin woman, living in constant terror of her husband. Promised court protection, she lost some of her fear and began to unburden herself as to her knowledge of the case.

"My husband was away from home on the night of September 21 and didn't get back until after four the next morning," she admitted.

"What was his appearance that morning?" asked Detective Hufford. "Did he seem nervous or excited?"

"He had a bad cut on his leg and was very jumpy. I dressed the wound, and he threatened that if I ever spoke of his being away during the night he would kill me."

"Did you ever see him with a hatchet?"

"Yes," she replied. "He kept one around the barn. I saw him grinding it a few days before this thing happened, but I haven't seen it since."

"Could you tell me if this is the one he had?" asked Detective Hufford, taking out the weapon found in the ruins.

After close scrutiny during which she turned it over and over in her frail hands, she replied, "I don't know of any marks by which I could identify it, but I feel quite sure that this is my husband's hatchet."

Then a domestic in the Little home, Mary Lee, was questioned. She stated that she had gone to the barn on the evening of September 22 and had seen Little counting a roll of bills. When he saw her, he hurriedly left and went into the pasture. Men were sent out with instructions to search every foot of the pasture in an effort to find the money. Soon the hunt was centered on a pile of logs near the edge of the pasture field. One by one the logs were removed, but instead of finding the money, they found an interesting bit of evidence: a lantern splotched with blood. When this was turned over to Detective Hufford, it was learned that the lantern was the one that had been discarded at the barns of the W. M. Ritter Lumber Company. The barn foreman identified the lantern as one he had ordered thrown away.

"Do you know who took this lantern from the barn?"

"Yes," he answered. "We had a sick horse about two weeks before the killing, and I took this old lantern down to look the critter over. While I was doctoring it, the boys took a notion to have a game of stud poker. But the wick was just about gone, and it was sputtering and flaring, so I cut a wick from the brim of my old hat. It did very well, and we played till about midnight."

"What became of the lantern after the game?"

"Well, George Meadows had been playing with us, and when the game was over, he cut his initials on the old lantern and said he was going to take it home with him. I never saw it again until now."

"Is that the same hat you were wearing that night?" asked the detective, indicating a battered, wide-brimmed felt perched back on the man's head.

"Yes, it is," he replied.

From the old lantern, the detective extracted the ribbon of wick. It fit perfectly into the nick in the hat brim. The lantern had last been seen in the possession of George Meadows on the night he played poker at the logging camp. He had cut his initials on the oil basin with a knife and then taken it to Aunt Betty's house. It was next seen again on the premises of Howard Little. The letters on the basin had been scratched out with a file, and there were bloodstains on the base. This bit of circumstantial evidence seemed to show that Howard Little had entered the house of Aunt Betty to rob her of the $1,300.00 he had paid her for her timberland. After murdering the family, he had set fire to the house and had taken the lantern to light his way over the rough trail home. Realizing that it might incriminate him, he had secreted it in the pile of logs. But now it was to prove his undoing. Detective Hufford was convinced he had the right man and turned the evidence over to the State's attorney.

On November 27, 1909, the little gray stone courthouse at Grundy was jammed to capacity. Hill people from the surrounding communities flocked to the scene of the trial. The prisoner, who had maintained his innocence since the time of his arrest, was led to the bar.

A hush fell over the crowd as Judge G. W. Burns of the Buchanan County Circuit Court said, "Howard Little, you stand before this bar of justice, charged with murder in the first degree, which charge, if proved, carries with it a maximum penalty of death. Are you guilty or not guilty?"

Little's eyes looked hard at the judge. "Not guilty!" he said loudly.

The trial then got underway. Little was placed on the stand on his own behalf. When questioned about the revolver, he firmly declared that he had never owned a gun and had not used one for three years. Noah Stacy, who had been called by both the State and defense as a witness, was next put on the stand, and he repeated the story of loaning the gun to Little and of his returning it to his father with two empty shells in the chamber. The gun was then identified by McClanahan as the one that he had lost in West Virginia. The damning testimony of Mrs. Little and Mary Lee was the last to be heard. Then the defense counsel laid his plea before the jury. When he had completed his argument, States Attorney Samuel Kiser arose and wove a net around Howard Little from which he was never able to extricate himself.

The jury then took the case and retired to the jury room. After a short deliberation, a knock was heard at the door. Tensely the crowd waited while Judge Burns asked if they had arrived at a verdict. "We have, Your Honor," came the reply. They filed into the room, and the foreman handed to the clerk of the court the written verdict that was to decide Little's fate.

He arose and in a trembling voice read, "We, the jury, do find the defendant guilty of murder in the first degree."

No mercy was recommended. This meant that Howard Little must die. Again Judge Burns faced the prisoner.

"Howard Little," he said, "you have been found guilty of murder in the first degree by a jury of twelve men, and as the Buchanan County Jail is deemed unsafe, I demand that you be taken to the Roanoke County Jail at Roanoke, Virginia, and there be placed in solitary confinement until such time as you may be removed to the State Penitentiary at Richmond. And there on the seventh day of February, 1910, between the hours of six o'clock in the morning and six o'clock in the evening you shall be placed in the electric chair and electrocuted until you are dead."

A two-day respite was granted by Governor Claude Swanson of Virginia, and the date of execution was fixed for February 9. At seven thirty in the morning, Little was led to the death chamber. He retained his composure as he took his seat in the death chair. Everyone waited for the confession, but none came. As the helmet was being adjusted, he closed his eyes and his lips parted. "Lord have mercy on an innocent man," he said. At that instant, a switch was closed. A mighty current surged through the body of Howard Little as he paid the penalty for the most brutal crime ever committed in the Cumberland Mountains.

The above information from the *Master Detective* article, in my opinion, portrays with accuracy the events that led up to the murder; the circumstantial evidence that was gathered to charge, arrest, and indict Howard Little for the murders; and his conviction. The one piece of information not accurate is the date of Howard Little's execution. The Buchanan County Circuit Court Judge Burns had ordered his execution set for January 7, 1910. Governor Claude Swanson respited the execution until February 11, 1910, and at 7:30 a.m. on this morning, the execution of Howard Little was carried out at the Richmond State Penitentiary. He was thirty-eight years old. Copies of these documents from the Library of Virginia were used for verification purposes. I have included in this book a picture of Howard Little taken during his incarceration at the Richmond State Penitentiary. I believe this picture was taken shortly before his execution. The source of this picture is also from the Library of Virginia.

The following information comes courtesy of the Buchanan County Virginia Circuit Court Grand Jury Indictment.

> On November 16, 1909, the Buchanan County Grand Jury was convened. Members of the grand jury were John A. Cook, Foreman; Floyd McClanahan; George W. Stiltner; Wiley O'Quin; Lilburn Fields; Jacob R. Presley; Mathias Keen; Robert Combs; Richard Yates; George W. McClanahan; and John

May. These members were sworn in a Grand Jury of Inquest and, having received their charge, were sent out of the court and shortly returned into the court with an indictment against Howard Little for felony murder. The jury, upon their oath, determined that Howard Little did feloniously, willfully, and of malice aforethought kill and murder against the peace and dignity of the Commonwealth of Virginia. In the official indictment, it states, "Upon the evidence of P. L. Johnson and Mary Lee, witnesses sworn in open court and sent to the grand jury to give evidence." Therefore, a True Bill was returned by John A. Cook, Foreman.

On November 25, 1909, an Indictment for Felony against Howard Little was presented. According to official documents, the court was not able to obtain a panel of sixteen jurors from those summoned, and in attendance upon the court, the court directed another venire facias to be issued and caused to be summoned from the list furnished by the court a number sufficient to complete the panel, and the sheriff having returned the writ of venire facias, together with the names of sixteen qualified jurors, free from exceptions, being completed and the prisoner having stricken from the said panel four of the said jurors, the remaining twelve constituted the jury for the trial of the prisoner, to wit: James W. Nickels, A. G. Arms, Alex Murphy, Benjamin C. Childress, David Deel, W. S. Ellis, William A. Ratliff, Arch T. Ratliff, J. H. McGlothlin, C. P.

Vandikes, G. C. Addison, and R. W. Perkins, who were sworn the truth of, and upon the premises to speak, and having particularly heard the evidence were given in charge of the sheriff, to whom was administered an oath that he would keep them together without communication with any person and that he would neither converse with them himself nor permit others to do so touching this trial. Howard Little was remanded to jail.

On November 27, 1909, the Circuit Court continued and held for Buchanan County, this day came again the Commonwealth by her attorney and the prisoner, Howard Little, by his attorney. The trial was held and witnesses presented by both the Commonwealth and the defense. Once the trial ended, the jury was sent to their room to consider their verdict and after some time returned into the court with the following verdict, to wit: "We, the jury, find the said Howard Little, guilty of murder in the first degree." Thereupon, the said prisoner, Howard Little, moved the court to set aside the verdict of the Jury, cause of misdirection of the court in permitting evidence to be introduced over the defendant's objection and in excluding evidence offered by the defendant, and because the verdict is contrary to law, and because said verdict is contrary to the evidence, which motion the court overruled, to which action of the court the defendant then accepted. Nothing further being offered in stay of the judgment and sentence of the court, it is now, therefore, considered by the court that the said Howard Little be taken to the jail of the City of Roanoke, Virginia, the jail of this county not being deemed sufficient, for his safe keeping therein, to be safely kept by the jailer of said City in solitary confinement until he is removed and caused to be conveyed to the Penitentiary of Virginia in the manner provided by law, and that the Superintendent of said penitentiary or his assistants appointed by him, shall, on Friday, the 7th day of January, 1910, between the hours of 6 o'clock a.m. and 6 o'clock p.m. of that day proceed to have, or cause, the said Howard Little to be electrocuted until he is dead, in the manner and by the means provided by law.

Additionally, I've included the "Order Transferring Prisoner" from the Buchanan County Virginia Circuit Court.

Order Transferring Prisoner

The jail of Buchanan County, Virginia, not being sufficient or safe, and the court not considering it safe to keep Howard Little, who has been convicted of murder in the first degree, and sentenced, at the present term of this court, it is ordered that the Sheriff of this county cause said Howard Little to be safely delivered, by the hands of C. W. McCoy, Keen Bevins, P. L. Johnson, Sam Baker, and Riley Lester, members of the guard appointed by an order entered at the prior day of the present term of this court, to the jail of the City of Roanoke, Virginia, in custody of the jailer thereof, to be by him safely kept until he shall be removed or caused to be removed by the Superintendent of the Penitentiary of Virginia, to be electrocuted under the sentence of this court, as shown by its order, a copy of which duly certified, together with a copy of this order duly certified, with the seal of this court attached, to each shall be delivered to the jailer of the said City of Roanoke, which shall be his authority for receiving said Howard Little. A true transcript. Signed by Jo Hibbitts, Clerk.

Included in this book is a picture of the court-ordered deputies surrounding the prisoner, believed to have been taken at the Raven Depot Train Station, upon their boarding the train to take the prisoner to the Roanoke City Jail. A note of interest: One of the deputies, Sam Baker, was Aunt Betty's son-in-law, married to her daughter, Pricy Jane. He was a deputized sheriff's officer for the Hurley area.

Upon the executive order signed by Governor Claude Swanson (copy included in this book), Howard Little was executed on February 11, 1910. The Commonwealth of Virginia began executions by electrocution in 1908. Howard Little was prisoner number twenty-three executed in Virginia.

Aunt Betty, Lydia, and her three small sons, Will, Noah, and Lafayette, are buried in one grave in the Justus Cemetery on Laurel Creek. I have included a picture of the grave, a huge monument. George Meadows is buried beside them. During the investigation, George Meadows's body was exhumed to further examine the bullet wounds to determine a match to the gun, which was a large part of the circumstantial evidence against Howard Little. My great-grandfather, Hiram Wylie Justus, is buried near the common grave.

In author Sam Varney's book, *Appalachian Lore and Legend*, he devoted a chapter about this murder entitled "The Story of Howard Little." This was enlightening to me because he included court documents of Howard Little's arrest and trial. Another magazine, *Inside Detective*, dated October 1944, included an article of the murders entitled "100% Villain," written by David Robinson George. This story is told from the perspective of Buchanan County Sheriff Norton Brewster and his Chief Deputy Phineas Tallman. The article does not mention Detective A. C. Hufford being involved in the investigation. I am not certain if the information in this article is entirely factual. From all sources, it appears that Detective Hufford was the lead investigator in the case.

For God shall bring every work into judgment, with every secret thing, whether it be good, or whether it be evil.

Ecclesiastes 12:14 KJV

Elizabeth Baker Justus Sketch from the
Master Detective Magazine July, 1935.

(Right) Grandma Polly Justus Charles, daughter of
Elizabeth Baker Justus. (Left) Grandma Polly's daughter,
Pearlie Charles Blankenship. Family Photograph.

Lumber Mill at Hurley about 1909

W. M. Ritter Lumber Company from 1909. Family Photograph.

Town of Grundy, Virginia, about 1912. Public Photograph.

Christmas Eve fire 1915, Courthouse and most of town devastated.

Buchanan County, Virginia Courthouse,
about 1915. Public Photograph.

Buchanan County, Virginia Courthouse today. Public Photograph.

Buchanan County, Virginia Sign at Shortts Gap. Public Photograph.

Buchanan County, Virginia Sign at Shortts Gap. Public Photograph.

VIRGINIA:

    COUNTY OF BUCHANAN, to-wit:

    Please before the Circuit Court of the County of Buchanan, at the Court House of the said County, on the 27th day of November, 1909.

    Be it remembered, That heretofore, to-wit: At a Circuit Court, held for the said County, at the Court-house, on the 15th day of November, 1909, John A. Cook, Foreman, Floyd McClanahan, Geo. W. Stiltner, (of Fred), Wiley Rippett O'quin, Lilburn Fields, Jacob R. Presley, Mathias Keen, Robert Combs, Richard Yates, George W. McClanahan, and John May, were sworn a Grand Jury of Inquest, in and for the body of the County of Buchanan, and having received their charge, were sent out of Court, and after sometime returned into court with an indictment against Howard Little, for Felony, which with the endorsement thereon by the Foreman, is as follows:

              INDICTMENT.

Commonwealth of Virginia, xxxxxxxxx Buchanan County, to-wit:

    In the Circuit Court of said County:

    The Jurors of the Grand Jury, in and for the County aforesaid, empaneled and sworn at the term thereof, commencing on the 15th day of November, 1909, and now attending said Court, upon their oath present, that Howard Little, on the ___ day of _____, 190°, in said County, with force and arms, in and upon the body of one George Meadows, in the peace of said Commonwealth, then and there being, feloniously, wilfully, and of his malice aforethought, did make an assault, and the said Howard Little, a certain pistol, then and there charged with gun powder and leaden bullets, which said pistol, he, the said Howard Little, in his hand then and there had and held, then and there feloniously, wilfully, and of his malice aforethought, did discharge and shoot of to, against and upon the body of the said George Meadows, and the said Howard Little,

Buchanan County, Virginia Circuit Court.
Howard Little Indictment for Felony Murder
Courtesy of the Library of Virginia.

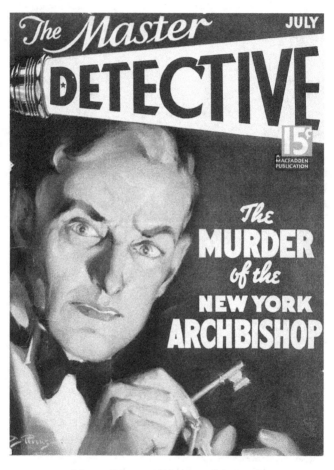

Master Detective Magazine July, 1935.

THE
MASTER DETECTIVE

A MACFADDEN PUBLICATION ★ VOL. ★ 12 ★ NO. ★ 5

JULY 1935

COVER BY DALTON STEVENS

PUBLISHED MONTHLY BY MACFADDEN PUBLICATIONS, INC., WASHINGTON AND SOUTH AVENUES, DUNELLEN, NEW JERSEY
Editorial and General Offices: 1926 Broadway, New York, N. Y.   Advertising Offices: Graybar Building, New York City
Bernarr Macfadden, President   Wesley F. Pape, Secretary   I. T. Kennedy, Treasurer   William Terry, Advertising Director
Copyright, 1935, by Macfadden Publications, Inc., Copyright also in Canada and Great Britain.
Entered as Second Class Matter July 16, 1999, at the Post Office at Dunellen, N. J., under the Act of March 3, 1879. Additional entry at New York, N. Y. Price 15c
per Copy in U. S.—10c in Canada. Subscription price $1.50 per year in the United States and possessions; also Cuba, Mexico and Panama. (Canada, $2.40 per year.) All
other countries $3.00 per year. All rights reserved.
Chicago Office: 333 N. Michigan Ave., C. H. Shattuck, Mgr. London Agents: Atlas Publishing & Distributing Co., Ltd., 18 Bride Lane, London, E. C. Contributors are ad-
vised to retain copies of their contributions. Every effort will be made by us to return unavailable manuscripts, photographs and drawings (if accompanied by first-class postage),
but we will not be responsible for any losses of such matter contributed. The pictures used in this magazine to illustrate the stories are of actual people, but are not intended
to be a likeness of, nor to depict, the individuals named in such stories, unless such pictures are specifically labeled.

Master Detective Magazine July, 1935. Table of Contents,
reference article "Capturing the Killer of the Cumberlands."

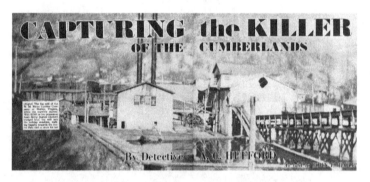

Master Detective Magazine July, 1935. Article,
"Capturing the Killer of the Cumberlands."

Master Detective Magazine July, 1935. Detective A. C. Hufford

Inside Detective Magazine October, 1944.

CONTENTS

OCTOBER, 1944

INSIDE **detective**

West Peterson, Editor

Carlos Lane, Betty Gleason, Associate Editors   Otto Storch, Art Director

Cover Kodachrome by Pagano

INSIDE DETECTIVE is a periodical for the dissemination of technical information and crime-prevention news to police officers, county coroners, district attorneys, and jurists.

POSTMASTER: Please send notice on Form 3578, and copies returned under Label Form 3579 to 149 Madison Avenue, New York 16, New York.

INSIDE DETECTIVE, Volume 20 No. 4, October, 1944. Copyright, 1944, by W. Peterson. Published monthly. Office of publication at Washington and South Avenues, Dunellen, N. J. Executive, editorial and subscription offices, 149 Madison Avenue, New York 16, N. Y. Chicago advertising office, 360 N. Michigan Avenue, Chicago 1, Ill. Printed in the U. S. A. Single copy price ten cents. Subscription in the United States $1.00 a year, foreign subscription $2.20 a year. Entered as second class matter January 15, 1935, at the Post Office at Dunellen, N. J., under the Act of March 3, 1879. The publisher accepts no responsibility for the return of unsolicited material. All manuscripts should be accompanied by stamped, self-addressed envelope.

Inside Detective Magazine October, 1944.
Table of Contents, reference article, "100% Villain."

Inside Detective Magazine October, 1944. Article "100% Villain."

Commonwealth of Virginia,

To all to Whom These Presents Shall Come--Greeting:

WHEREAS, at a *Circuit* Court held in and for the *County* of *Buchanan* in the month of *November*, in the year one thousand *nine* hundred and *nine* *Howard Little* was convicted of *murder in the first degree*, and was thereupon sentenced to be *hanged* on the *fourth* day of *January*, one thousand nine hundred and *ten*, and whereas it appears to the Executive that it is proper that the execution of said sentence be temporarily suspended:

THEREFORE, I, **CLAUDE A. SWANSON,** Governor of the Commonwealth of Virginia, have, by virtue of authority vested in me, respited and do hereby respite the execution of the said sentence until the *eleventh* day of *February*, one thousand nine hundred and *ten*, and do order that on the said last-named day the sentence of the said court be duly executed.

Given under my hand and under the Lesser Seal of the Commonwealth, at Richmond, this *21st* day of *December*, in the year of our Lord, one thousand nine hundred and *nine* and in the one hundred and thirty *fourth* year of the Commonwealth.

Claude A. Swanson

By the Governor:

B. O. James
Secretary of the Commonwealth.

Governor Claude Swanson signs respite order of
execution. Courtesy Library of Virginia.

The Penitentiary
RICHMOND, VA.

February 11, 1910.

Clerk, Circuit Court,

Buchanan County Virginia.

This is to certify that the order of the Circuit Court of Buchanan County, dated November 27, 1909, directing the electrocution of Howard Little on January 7, 1910, between the hours of 6 o'clock A. M. and 6 o'clock P. M., the execution of which was respited until February 11, 1910, by the Governor of the Commonwealth, was this day executed at 7.30 A. M.

Superintendent.

Order of execution carried out by The Penitentiary,
Richmond, Virginia on February 11, 1910 at
7:30am. Courtesy Library of Virginia.

Virginia Governor Claude Swanson. Courtesy Library of Virginia.

Deputies transporting Howard Little to Roanoke,
Virginia Jail. Left to right: Keen Bevins, Sam Baker, Riley
Lester, Howard Little, Wallace McCoy, Lebanon Jailer
Gibson, Patt Johnson, and Bill Webb, a bystander.

Howard Little and wife, Mary Little. Family Photograph.

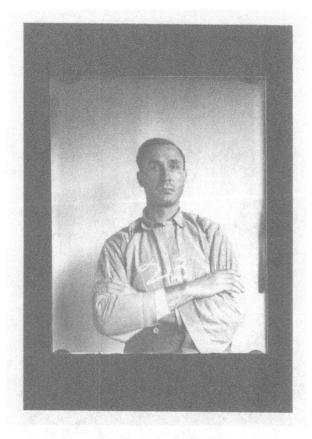

Howard Little photograph taken at The Penitentiary, Richmond, Virginia. He was the 23rd person to be executed by electrocution in Virginia since its inception. Picture taken just days before his execution. Courtesy Library of Virginia.

ON SEPTEMBER 21, 1909
BETWEEN THE HOURS OF 9:00
AND 10:00 P.M. AT A LOG CABIN
APPROXIMATELY 300 YARDS FROM
THIS PRESENT LOCATION, SIX PEOPLE
WERE BRUTALLY MURDERED.
THE MOTIVE WAS ROBBERY. ELIZABETH
JUSTUS, HER DAUGHTER LYDIA MEADOWS,
LYDIA'S THREE CHILDREN, WILL, NOAH AND
LAFAYETTE MEADOWS, WERE KILLED AND
REMAINED IN THE CABIN AS IT WAS SET ABLAZE.
LYDIA'S HUSBAND, GEORGE, WAS SHOT TWICE
AND HE DIED IN FRONT OF THE CABIN.
ON NOVEMBER 27, 1909, HOWARD LITTLE WAS
CONVICTED OF FIRST DEGREE MURDER AND ON
JANUARY 7, 1910 IN RICHMOND, VIRGINIA, HE
WAS PUT TO DEATH BY ELECTROCUTION IN
ACCORDANCE WITH THE COURTS SENTENCE.
IT IS BELIEVED THAT AFTER COMMITTING THESE
ACTS OF BRUTALITY, HOWARD LITTLE FLED UP
THE HOLLOW JUST TO THE RIGHT OF THIS
MONUMENT, TO HIS HOME WHERE HE WAS LATER
APPREHENDED.

Grave monument detailing the murders of Elizabeth
Baker Justus and her family. Family Photograph.

Grave marker of Elizabeth Baker Justus, Lydia Justus
Meadows, Will, Noah, and Lafayette Meadows. All
are buried in one grave. Family Photograph.

Grave marker of George Meadows. He was buried
beside the others. Family Photograph.

Grave monument (other side) detailing Hiram Wylie and
Elizabeth Baker Justus' children. Standing beside the monument
is the Author's daughter, Jamie Danielle Carty. She is a great-
great granddaughter of Elizabeth. Family Photograph.

Grave marker of Hiram Wylie Justus, husband of Elizabeth.
He is buried near the common grave. Family Photograph.

VIRGINIA STATE PENITENTIARY PHOTOGRAPH COLLECTION
C1: 151
1991
approx. 270 Kodak prints with negatives

Receiving its first prisoners in 1800, the Virginia State Penitentiary in Richmond had by the 1980s, through a series of radical redesigns, grown from architect Benjamin Latrobe's elegant horseshoe-shaped loggia on the banks of the James to an enormous modern complex of cellblocks and administrative buildings, mostly constructed with inmate labor, and partly from the brick and stone of Latrobe's original horseshoe, itself fallen into disuse and razed in 1928.

In 1991, with the inmate population decentralized and relocated to various facilities throughout the state, and the penitentiary buildings themselves doomed to obsolescence, the Virginia Film Office sent photographers to survey the complex as a potential movie location. While ultimately no movies were filmed in "the Pen," the photographers did gather the most comprehensive and intimate visual account of the penitentiary made near the end of its long life cycle, a year before its demolition by the state. The exterior and interior photos are rich in detail and include views of the dining hall, the chapel, and the infirmary with its distinctive green-and-white checkered floor, as well as glimpses along the inner lengths of the tiered cellblocks, various furniture, lamps, and other unexpected details of life behind bars, such as houseplants and an umbrella casually hung by its handle on an open door. One long panorama, composed of five separate snapshots, captures the penitentiary's high-walled athletic field in its entirety, and behind it the Richmond cityscape, with the Jefferson Hotel and City Hall easily distinguishable.

Early photograph of The Penitentiary, Richmond,
Virginia. Courtesy Library of Virginia.

The Commonwealth of Kentucky.

TO ANY SHERIFF, CONSTABLE, JAILER, MARSHAL OR POLICEMAN OF THIS STATE:

It appearing from the ~~oath or~~ an affidavit *On file in my office*

that there are reasonable grounds to believe that

Howard Little

ha_s_ committeed

the ~~offense~~ *crime of willful Murder*

Committed as follows: The said Howard Little did willfully, feloniously and of his malice afore-thought Kill and Murder Jacob Kinney by shooting him with a winchester rifle loaded with powder and ball.

on the *19th* day of *June* 189_2_ against the peace and dignity of the Commonwealth of Kentucky in the County of Pike, you are therefore commanded forthwith to arrest the said

Howard Little

at Pikeville

and bring *him* before me, ~~or some other Magistrate~~ of Pike county, to be dealt with according to law.

Given under my hand, as *Judge of the Pike County Court*

this the *7th* day of *July* 189_2_ *Bart Becker J.P.C.*

Summons as witnesses for the Commonwealth *Harve Mullins, John H. Mullins, John Mullins, Peggy Mullins, Jink Mullins, Alex Mullins sr. Ren Tackett & W.J. Roberts.*

The Defendant ~~may give bail in the sum of~~ *allowed no bail*

~~Dollars, for~~ ~~appearance on the~~ _day of_ 189_

Bart Becker

Arrest order for Howard Little for Felony Murder in the Commonwealth of Kentucky. Courtesy Kentucky Department of Libraries and Archives, Frankfort, Kentucky.

$_____ =REWARD=

ESCAPED FROM

= KENTUCKY PENITENTIARY =

Name   HOWARD LITTLE,

Crime   MURDER,

Sentence Life years. *County,* Pike,

Received. March 26, 1893,

Age 21 *years.* *Height* 6 *feet* 3/4 *inches.* *Weight* 176

Color of eyes   Blue   *Color of hair* Dark

Complexion   Fair,

Trade   Laborer,

Marks and Scars: Scar outside left first finger;

scar and mole outside left hip;

Pardoned by Lieut. Gov. Worthington

March 25, 1898.

Above reward will be paid for delivery of said

to prison at

Frankfort, Ky

Order of Pardon of Howard Little from Kentucky Prison, signed by Lieutenant Governor Worthington, March 25, 1898. Courtesy Kentucky Department of Libraries and Archives, Frankfort, Kentucky.

Georgia (Blankenship) Robair-West, daughter of Amy
Caroline Justus, great-granddaughter of Elizabeth
Baker Justus. Courtesy of Mrs. Robair-West.

MORE MURDER

The arrest and conviction for these gruesome murders does not complete the story of Howard Little. During my search to gather information and factual documentation regarding this crime, I discovered, to my horror, that this was not the first time he had been convicted for murder. From the Department of Libraries and Archives in Frankfort, Kentucky, I uncovered the following information: Howard Little was charged with having committed the crime of willful murder. The indictment states that Howard Little did willfully, feloniously, and of malice aforethought kill and murder Jacob Kinney by shooting him with a Winchester rifle loaded with powder and ball on the nineteenth day of June, 1892, against the peace and dignity of the Commonwealth of Kentucky in the County of Pike. Witnesses for the Commonwealth were Harve Mullins, John H. Mullins, John Mullins, Peggy Mullins, Pink Mullins, Alex Mullins, Ben Tackett, and W. J. Roberts. A Warrant of Arrest was issued against Howard Little on July

26, 1892, by J. Lee Ferguson, Commonwealth Attorney for Pike County, Kentucky.

The details surrounding the circumstances of this murder are scarce. The documents from the courts are handwritten and very difficult to read; however, the best I can determine is that there was an argument and/or altercation between Jacob Kinney and Howard Little that resulted in Howard Little murdering Jacob Kinney by shooting him. Parts of the documents indicate that the United States Marshalls were attempting to serve papers on Jacob Kinney for violation of the United States Internal Revenue laws, and he refused to accept them. Some Kentucky newspapers have referred to Howard Little as being a US Marshall. The documents seem to indicate that Howard Little was assisting the Marshalls to serve the papers on Jacob Kinney. At some point, there was an altercation and Jacob Kinney was killed.

Howard Little, by his attorney A. W. Harkins, claimed self-defense in the murder, stating that he feared for his life, that Jacob Kinney intended to kill him, and he defended himself. Julia Mullins, a witness for the defense, stated that the day before the shooting, Jacob Kinney stated to her that if he went to prison and was released, he would hunt Howard Little down and kill him. In the end, Howard Little was convicted of murder on March 26, 1893. I obtained the document, the Register of Convicts from the Kentucky Penitentiary, and it documents that Howard Little was convicted of murder in Pike County Circuit Court and was sentenced to life in prison.

I was further amazed to discover a document of pardon signed by Kentucky Lieutenant Governor Worthington dated March 25, 1898. Yes, Howard Little was pardoned and released from prison after serving exactly five years for the murder of Jacob Kinney. On September 21, 1909, eleven years and six months after his release from the Kentucky Penitentiary, he murdered an entire family.

I cannot end this book without discussing another murder that occurred in the aftermath of the Justus and Meadows family massacre. Samuel Baker, son-in-law of Aunt Betty, was shot and killed in December, 1909, by Henry Pennington. The story goes that Sam and Pricy Baker were walking out of Laurel Creek to attend a Christmas Eve party in Hurley at the Ritter Lumber Company. The story handed down through the generations says that Henry Pennington was dating a young girl named Rose who was living with Sam and Pricy Baker during this time.

The story goes that Henry Pennington was walking up Laurel Creek to meet Rose, and on the way, he met Sam and Pricy walking down the road. An argument ensued between Sam and Henry. It is possible that Sam and Pricy did not approve of Pennington, as he reputedly had a bad reputation in the Hurley community. Another story goes that Rose was also dating Wyatt Meadows and that Wyatt Meadows was with Sam and Pricy walking down Laurel Creek.

We will never really know what started the argument, but the fact is that Jason Pennington shot and killed Samuel

Baker. Pricy Baker took Sam's gun and shot at Pennington and shot him twice but did not kill him. Henry Pennington shot Pricy in the hip, and she was seriously wounded but did survive. Pennington ran off into the woods and got away for a while. Later a lynch mob went after Pennington, and when they found him, he was tied to a steam pipe at the Ritter Lumber Company and lynched. After he was lynched, people shot his body full of holes. This was on Christmas Eve 1909, and it was bitterly cold. The story goes that Pennington's body was left for several days for all to see. I have heard that his blood turned into icicles from where he was left hanging. He body was eventually taken down. I do not know who took him down or where they took the body for burial.

O Lord, our Lord, How excellent is Your name in all the earth!

Psalm 8:9 KJV

Below is the newspaper article from the *Times Dispatch (later the Richmond Times Dispatch)*, dated Monday, December 27, 1909:

Hurley Murderer Lynched by Mob
Henry Pennington Hanged and
Body Riddled with Bullets
Victim Slain on Christmas Eve
Wife of Sam Baker Seeks Vengeance
and Is Wounded
Tragic Outcome of Little's Sextuple Murders
First Virginia Lynching in Four Years

Following the killing here on Christmas Eve of Samuel Baker and the serious wounding of his wife and two children by the former's enemy, Henry Pennington, a mob of one hundred citizens late last night took Henry Pennington from an improvised jail, where he had been incarcerated under heavy guard, and hanged him to a steam pipe.

Pennington, who had been drinking, picked a quarrel with Baker and shot him while the latter was on his way to a Sunday School Christmas Tree event with his wife and two children and a friend, Wyatt Meadows. Seeing that he had killed Baker, Pennington started to run away. Mrs. Baker called after Pennington and implored him to help her take the body home. The ruse worked and Pennington went back to the spot where his victim lay dead. Bent upon avenging the dead, Mrs. Baker grabbed

Pennington's pistol from his pocket and shot twice at him. Her aim was bad, but she succeeded in wounding him in the hand and thigh. Pennington recovered possession of the pistol and then shot the woman and attempted to kill Meadows, who was running away, and the two children.

Pennington then fled but was surrounded by a posse on the outskirts of the town later in the night. He was captured after an exchange of shots with the officers, who badly wounded him. Being too weak to stand the journey to the Grundy Jail (15 miles distant over mountainous country), Pennington was locked up in the constable's home, but about one o'clock yesterday it was thought advisable to remove him to a boarding house, where he was put under a strong guard. Feeling against Pennington ran high and many covert threats of lynching were heard during the day. Last midnight a band of about 100 citizens was quietly organized. The guard was overpowered, and Pennington was taken to the engine room of a lumber mill nearby and hanged to a steam pipe. The body was riddled with bullets and was then left hanging until 9 o'clock this morning when it was cut down. Baker's funeral was held today but his wife was too badly wounded to attend. Baker was a son-in-law of Aunt Betty Justus and brother-in-law of George Meadows, two of the victims of the famous sextuple murders here several months ago for which Howard Little has been sentenced to die in the electric chair on January 6th.

Pennington was known to be a friend of Howard Little and it is thought that the talk of a new trial for Little had much to do with his seeking a quarrel with Baker, and as well for the sentiment which provoked the lynching which followed. Little has been granted a 30-day respite by Governor Swanson, his attorney's claiming that his witnesses were intimidated by the friends of the Meadows' family and that he has been sentenced because of his previous bad reputation with no evidence other than circumstantial.

The lynching in Buchanan County of Henry Pennington is the first affair of this kind during the administration of Governor Swanson. For more than four years the State has been free from any lawlessness of this sort.

Buchanan County has no railroad and mail and telephone service is exceedingly slow and unsatisfactory. Not even the news of Pennington's crime had reached Governor Swanson until he was apprised last night of the lynching. Even had the Buchanan County Sheriff anticipated trouble and had been able to communicate immediately after the crime with the executive, no militia could have reached the scene in time to prevent the trouble. There is now no militia company west of Lynchburg and two or three days would elapse before any soldiers could reach the mountain fastness of the Kentucky border.

From what I have discovered, after the murder of Samuel Baker, Rose eventually married Wyatt Meadows and raised several children, including Rose's child by Henry Pennington.

One evening I was invited to dinner with Georgia (Blankenship) Robair-West and a dear friend, Josephine (Hall) Blankenship, at Georgia's lovely home. Georgia had commented to me previously that we were related, and I was interested to learn the connection. During the dinner conversation, Georgia relayed that Rose was, in fact, Pricy Baker's niece. Rose was Aunt Betty's granddaughter, the daughter of Aunt Betty's daughter, Amy Caroline. Georgia Robair-West is a granddaughter of Amy Caroline. Her father, Tom Blankenship, was Amy Caroline's son. I discovered, to my delight, that Georgia and I are both great-granddaughters of Aunt Betty (and both of us with the same name)!

In writing this book, I have fulfilled a life-long desire to memorialize my great-grandmother Elizabeth and her family. They were wonderful people living and enjoying a peaceful life surrounded by their family and friends. Even though it has been over one hundred years since their murders, and though I never knew them, their lives and deaths remain with me, and I often dwell on what happened to bring such a tragic end to their lives.

Take heed that ye despise not one of these little ones; for I say unto you, That in heaven their angels do always behold the face of my Father which is in heaven.

Matthew 18:10 KJV

Elizabeth Baker was born in April 1843 in Pike County, Kentucky. She died September 21, 1909, in Buchanan County, Virginia, Laurel Creek (Hurley). She was the daughter of Elijah Baker, born 1802, Caldwell, Kentucky, and died in 1862, Mill Creek, Buchanan County, Virginia, and Sarah (Polley) Baker, born 1806, Adair, Kentucky, died June 28, 1864, in Mill Creek, Buchanan County, Virginia. (Stories from family descendants indicate that Elijah Baker was a full-blooded Cherokee Indian.)

Hiram Wylie Justus was born October 15, 1837, in Tazewell County, Virginia, and died February 21, 1903, in Buchanan County, Virginia, Laurel Creek (Hurley). Hiram was a Private in the US Army during the Civil War (Wells Co Smiths BN VA CAV, Confederate States Army).

Hiram Wylie Justus and Elizabeth (Baker) Justus were married March 8, 1860.

Children of Hiram Wylie and Elizabeth (Baker) Justus:

Matilda Justus, infant born 1860, died 1860, Buchanan County, Virginia

William MacDaniel (Daniel) Justus, born July 11, 1861; died March 18, 1929, Buchanan County, Virginia (Laurel Creek)

Amy Caroline (Justus) Blankenship, born 1863; died 1900, Buchanan County, Virginia

Mary Polly (Justus) Charles, born May 5, 1865; died November 4, 1947, Buchanan County, Virginia

Morgan Justus, born May 17, 1868; died January 7, 1947, Buchanan County, Virginia

Samuel Senna Justus, born 1870; died 1943, Buchanan County, Virginia

Alfred Justus, born 1872; died February 4, 1890, Buchanan County, Virginia

James Justus, born October 1874; died August 9, 1905, Buchanan County, Virginia

Lafayette Justus, born March 5, 1876; died July 5, 1922, Buchanan County, Virginia

Pricy Jane (Justus) Baker, born July 2, 1878; died April 27, 1967, Buchanan County, Virginia

Andrew Justus, born May 14, 1884; died October 17, 1959, Buchanan County, Virginia

Lydia (Justus) Meadows, born December 1887; died September 21, 1909, Buchanan County, Virginia (Laurel Creek)

BIBLIOGRAPHY

Bailey, John. "Capturing the Killer of the Cumberlands." July 1935, 42-46.

George, David. "100% Villain." Inside Detective, October 1944, 24-26, 51.

Varney, Samuel. Appalachian Lore and Legend. 2004.

"Grand Jury Indictment." Buchanan County Virginia Court Document (1909): n.pag. Library of Virginia. Database.

"Hurley Murderer Lynched by Mob." Times Dispatch, December 27, 1909.

"Order Transferring Prisoner." Buchanan County Virginia Circuit Court (1909): n.pag. Library of Virginia. Database.

"Pike County Kentucky Circuit Court." Grand Jury Indictment (1892): n.pag. Department of Libraries and Archives Frankfort Kentucky. Database.

CPSIA information can be obtained
at www.ICGtesting.com
Printed in the USA
LVHW021559220419
615090LV00021B/829

9 781947 825611